NATIONAL GEOGRAPHIC

What Makes Me Healthy?

Nat Sui

I need good food to be healthy. Eating many kinds of foods each day helps me to be healthy.

What else do I need to be healthy?

I need water to be healthy. Drinking lots of clean, fresh water helps me to be healthy.

What else do I need to be healthy?

I need exercise to be healthy.
Exercising every day helps me
to be healthy.

What else do I need to be healthy?

I need sleep to be healthy.
Getting lots of sleep helps me
to be healthy.

What else do I need to be healthy?

I need people to care for me
to be healthy.
People who love me help me
to be healthy.

What do I need to be healthy?

I need all of these things to be healthy

food

exercise

sleep

water

love